THE SAVINGS SQUIRREL

A CHILDREN'S BOOK ABOUT UNDERSTANDING WHERE MONEY COMES FROM, SAVING, AND KNOWING THE VALUE OF A DOLLAR

WRITTEN BY CHARLOTTE DANE

ILLUSTRATED BY ADAM RIONG

THE SAVINGS SQUIRREL

This is Andy Squirrel and his best friend, Quincy Squirrel. They just love biking together.

Andy Squirrel

Quincy: "Aw, I'll never get them then! I'm going home. See you tomorrow at work."

Andy and Quincy worked collecting acorns for Squirrelburg.

Andy :"Hey Quincy, I want to tell you about how I got my bike. I paid for it myself, did you know that?"

Quincy: "I didn't know that! But it's so nice."
Andy: "It cost 20 acorns."

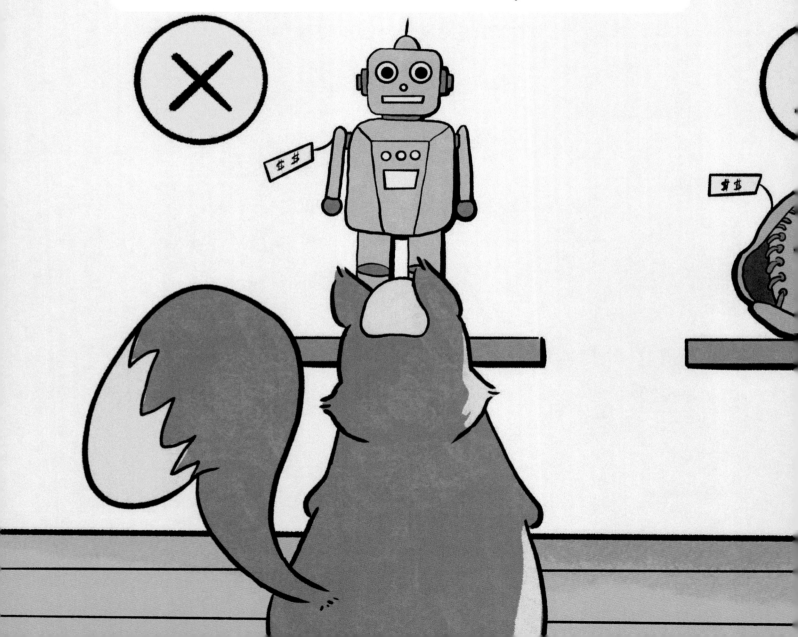

Andy: "We earn 5 acorns a week at work.
Let's make a chart! I'll show you."

Quincy thinking to himself "I already have shoes, but I want the new bike! Okay, decision is made and I'm going to stick to it!"

5 weeks later, the toy store brought over the new bike, and Quincy was so happy!

Andy: "Saving and budgeting means you can do what you want. Come on, let's go explore!"

Made in the USA
Monee, IL
04 February 2021